EXILE

AND OTHER POEMS

EXILE
AND OTHER POEMS

RICHARD ALDINGTON

with an introduction and notes by

ELIZABETH VANDIVER
&
VIVIEN WHELPTON

RENARD PRESS

RENARD PRESS LTD

124 City Road
London EC1V 2NX
United Kingdom
info@renardpress.com
020 8050 2928

www.renardpress.com

Exile and Other Poems first published in 1923
This edition first published by Renard Press Ltd in 2023

Exile and Other Poems © the Estate of Richard Aldington
Introduction and Notes © Elizabeth Vandiver and Vivien Whelpton, 2023

Cover design by Will Dady

Printed in the United Kingdom by Severn

ISBN: 978-1-80447-070-1

9 8 7 6 5 4 3 2 1

CLIMATE POSITIVE Renard Press is proud to be a climate positive publisher, removing more carbon from the air than we emit and planting a small forest. For more information see renardpress.com/eco.

The right of Richard Aldington to be identified as the author of this work in accordance with the Copyright, Designs and Patents Act 1988 has been asserted.

All rights reserved. This publication may not be reproduced, stored in a retrieval system or transmitted, in any form or by any means – electronic, mechanical, photocopying, recording or otherwise – without the prior permission of the publisher.

CONTENTS

Introduction	7
Exile and Other Poems	23
I. EXILE	25
Exile	27
Eumenides	29
Le Maudit	32
Bones	34
Meditation	37
In the Palace Garden	39
Epitaph in Ballade Form	41
At a Gate by the Way	43
Rhapsody in a Third-Class Carriage	45
Freedom	47
Retreat	49
Having Seen Men Killed	51
Nightingale	52
Papillons	54
Truth	55
To Those Who Played for Safety in Life	57

II. WORDS FOR MUSIC ... 59

Songs for Puritans: ... 61
- I ... 61
- II ... 62
- III ... 63
- IV ... 64
- V ... 65
- VI ... 66
- VII ... 67
- VIII ... 68
- IX ... 69
- X ... 70

Songs for Sensualists: ... 71
- A Sophistry of Duration ... 71
- A Garden Homily ... 72
- Words for Music ... 73
- Madrigal ... 74
- From Tasso ... 75

Metrical exercises: ... 76
- The Berkshire Kennet ... 76
- A Winter Night ... 81

Notes ... 85

INTRODUCTION

Ben Shepherd tells us that the doctors of the First World War came to realise that 'a man's capacity to endure in war was determined by many things – heredity, upbringing, "character", the society he came from, how he felt about the war, his relationship to his fellow soldiers, the length of time he had been fighting, whether his wife had been unfaithful – quite apart from the military circumstances in which he found himself.'* The influences that affected Richard Aldington's 'capacity to endure' were manifold.

He had grown up in dysfunctional family circumstances. His father, a solicitor, was naïve and ineffective, and his unwise investments led to bankruptcy on two occasions; along with the public humiliation, this meant the curtailment of Richard's education, both when he was removed from public day school at the age of thirteen and later, when he had to leave University College London after the first year of an undergraduate course. While he spent his whole life remedying his lack of a formal education, Aldington also felt the need to dissemble about it and often implied that he had received a typical public-school and university education. His mother was a much stronger character, from humbler roots, self-centred and a sensualist, who came to despise her weaker husband. Their son's portraits of his parents in *Death of a Hero* (1929) and *Very Heaven* (1937) are savage but not entirely false. Attachment theory is a useful tool for understanding his psychological vulnerability in later life and, particularly, his inability to form a lasting marital attachment.

Indeed, his marital problems contributed to the isolation and depression he experienced throughout his war service and into the decade that followed. In the brief pre-war period when he had found his vocation as a poet and a founder of the Imagist movement, a literary circle in which he could flourish, a partner and later wife, the American poet Hilda Doolittle (H.D.), whom he admired and adored, and a role as assistant editor of the journal *The Egoist*, Aldington had thrived. War disrupted it all and was even blamed (by H.D.) for the traumatic experience – for them both – of a stillborn child in May 1915. Their physical relationship suffered in the aftermath. By 1916 conscription was on the horizon and the prospect terrified him; he sought solace in a brief extra-marital affair. By March 1918, with his second period of service at the front looming, he was immersed in a far more passionate and emotionally serious affair. In a state of misery, H.D. left London for Cornwall and the company of the composer Cecil Gray, by whom she became pregnant. Aldington was unable to cope with the notion of this child replacing the one they had lost and was torn between H.D. and his lover, Dorothy Yorke, and the couple separated in April 1919, shortly after the birth of H.D.'s daughter. Aldington would spend the next nine years with Yorke in the Berkshire countryside.

His war experience is vividly recreated in *Death of a Hero* (1929) and in his collection of short stories *Roads to Glory*

(1930). After a period of training which he found utterly humiliating, he reached the Loos sector of the Western Front in January 1917. His battalion, the Eleventh Leicesters, were the Pioneers of Sixth Division – units whose tasks were to construct trenches, roads and railways, but also to serve as infantry when required to do so. The surroundings were grim, the ground dominated by slagheaps, mine works, industrial buildings and villages that were now masses of rubble. Work as a pioneer was taxing and the rear areas where they were billeted were under constant shell fire and intermittent gas bombardments. Aldington returned to England to undertake officer training in May and did not return to the front until nearly a year later, in the aftermath of the 1918 German Spring Offensive, by then commissioned as a second-lieutenant in the Ninth Battalion of the Royal Sussex Regiment.

The battalion was initially stationed in the same sector which he had left in the spring of 1917. In *Death of a Hero* he describes walking over the notorious Hill 70, captured by the Canadian corps while he was in England:

> At dawn one morning when it was misty he walked over the top of Hill 91 [Hill 70], where probably nobody had been by day since its capture. The heavy mist brooded about him in a strange stillness. Scarcely a sound on their immediate front, though from north and south came the vibration of furious drum-fire. The ground was a desert of shell-holes and torn rusty wire, and everywhere lay skeletons in steel helmets, still clothed in the rags of sodden khaki or field grey. Here a fleshless hand still clutched a broken rusty rifle; there a gaping, decaying boot showed the thin, knotty foot-bones. [...] Alone in the white curling mist, drifting slowly past like

wraiths of the slain, with the far-off thunder of drum-fire beating the air, Winterbourne stood in frozen silence and contemplated the last achievements of civilised men.*

These images would haunt him for a long time. Meanwhile, he became an acting company commander. Now that the Germans had exhausted their reserves, the Allied advance to victory began; but in late August Aldington was sent on a six-week signals course, re-joining his battalion as its signals officer on the 8th of October to take part in the final battle of the Hindenburg Line, the Battle of Cambrai. In a period of intense mobile warfare, the retreating German army putting up a stiff resistance, the battalion captured villages to the north-east of the town and participated on the 4th of November in the advance across the River Rhonelle.

The Armistice came on the 11th of November, but Aldington's military service did not end, as the Ninth Sussex became part of the Army of Occupation. War-weary and in poor physical health, attempting to deal at a distance with the conflict he was experiencing between his love for H.D. and his passion for Yorke and with the emotional impact of H.D.'s pregnancy, having no employment to which to return and devoid of creative inspiration, Aldington sank into a depressed state. Demobilised in February 1919, he occupied a shabby London hotel for the rest of that year and desperately tried to earn money by writing journal articles; his one stroke of good fortune was his appointment as French critic for the *Times Literary Supplement*. His parting from H.D. in April was abrupt and acrimonious; she would always feel that his emotional state at the time had verged on insanity. He wrote to his close friend and fellow poet F.S. Flint:

INTRODUCTION

> What you say about my writing is most kind, but my friend, I am going through a really desperate crisis. I have serious doubts about my talent. Everything I've written, everything I am writing, seems to me bad, spoiled, foolish. My poems seem stupid; my prose cliché-ridden. I must carry on writing in order to live. But I've lost any confidence. It's awful. I blush each time I see my name printed on work I deem to be pathetic. [...] If I had your knowledge of French literature at least I could feel less ashamed of the work I do for the *Times*. But all my pleasure writing about French authors is ruined for me by the thought that there exist certainly several people who could fulfil this role with more skill and knowledge than me. To sum up, I look like someone taking advantage of the public. I'm nothing but a mediocre poet, and a less than mediocre critic.*

That this ran deeper than a lack of professional confidence is made clear by the following passage from the same letter: 'Two days ago I was strolling with a woman friend along the paths at Hampton Court. There were lilac and apple trees in blossom, wallflowers, all the trees were covered in fresh, fragile foliage, the birds were singing. I thought of your poem 'Fragment' and, I don't know why, but I was overcome with a great sadness. It was the immense futility of life that brought a lump to my throat and I had the awful thought that by escaping death in the war I have perhaps missed my true fate.'* He was deeply traumatised by his war experiences and suffering from the syndrome familiarly known as 'survivor's guilt'.

These feelings were accompanied by bitter resentment towards those who had not been combatants, many of whom had continued to have successful literary careers throughout the war. He told Clement Shorter, editor of *The Sphere*, 'I wonder if you realise what a gulf there is in my generation between the men who fought and those who didn't? It's a strain being with them; I feel as if I was calling across an enormous ravine to them. Of course I've got used to meeting them, but honestly I shrink from it. I can't quite tell you why, except perhaps that we others have seen all the misery & pain & hunger & despair & death of the world & they, in their comfortable England, have not.'*

Inevitably the depression began to manifest itself in physical symptoms, which in turn increased the sense of victimhood. He had written to the American poet Amy Lowell at the end of March: 'I don't expect non-combatants to understand; they can't. But you see I'm not at all well; my nerves have got into such a state that I have a sort of "sympathetic" neuralgia in my neck and arms; I sleep badly; I have a "trench throat" & cough; I have ague, directly I get cold.'* By August he was on the verge of a complete breakdown and in September he went off on his own for a walking holiday in the west of England. He told Lowell 'I had to go away. I had no holiday after demobilisation, the Govt. did not pay me my gratuity for three months & I had to work like a slave to keep going. The result was I nearly broke down mentally, though my physical health is excellent. Since I got back I have only been able to work three days a week; if I work more I get horrible pains in my head, due, people say, to a sort of deferred shellshock.'*

In December 1919 he left London for the Berkshire countryside, where Yorke joined him a year later and where he adopted a punishing routine of reading, translating and reviewing.* His diagnosis of the state of post-war Britain was also profoundly gloomy. For him it was a time 'when the whole of Europe is in an ungodly mess as a result of the war; when the most superficial observer must notice a sharp decline in general morals and manners; when even wealthy England is on the verge of bankruptcy; when almost the whole life of the nation has become commercialised; when art and artists are in a lamentable state of disorder and neglect.'* However, residing in the Berkshire countryside seems to have given him some peace: '[N]o rumble and roar of night-fighting, no shell-burst or rattle of machine-guns, no trampling and cursing of transport columns and working parties, no sinister sudden glare of Very lights showing a landscape bristling with barbed wire.'* Memories of the war and thoughts of what it had cost him, personally and artistically, were easier to put behind him – or to suppress – here, although as his poem 'Eumenides' shows such thoughts still broke through.

That war neurosis was common following the First World War did not make it easier to deal with. Nor did sharing their experiences necessarily help veterans. In *Life for Life's Sake* Aldington describes his attendance at a battalion reunion in 1919: 'With the end of the war the true reason for our old feeling of union was gone, and by trying to revive it we were flogging a dead horse. We were no longer one hundred per cent soldiers, but subtly and inevitably turning back into civilians, with different aims, hopes and antipathies.'*

The modern concept of Post-Traumatic Stress Disorder, contested though it has been since its formulation by the American Psychiatric Association in 1980, has helped sufferers to free themselves from a sense of failure and made families, communities and societies more accepting. In the end, however, there has to be a process of mental self-repair; *Exile* was Aldington's first substantial attempt to process the trauma of his experience in poetry, to that point his dominant creative form. That it did not resolve his problems is evidenced by the long poem *A Fool i' the Forest*, published two years later, and – at the end of the decade – his satirical novel, *Death of a Hero*, and short stories, *Roads to Glory*. The bitterness with which his war experience left him was still evident over twenty-five years later in his controversial biography of Lawrence of Arabia (1955). The horrors of war may have faded, but the sense of betrayal had not. *Exile*, nevertheless, remains a moving testimony to the deep, complex and long-term impact of war on combatants.

* * *

Composing verse had become problematic for Aldington. Apologetically sending Harriet Monroe, editor of *Poetry*, some poems in October 1919, he wrote 'No doubt you will be disappointed with them. But I think you'll know that they are real and that they expose a common psychology of the time, the "lostness" & bitterness of my generation... I am getting over this phase. I am hoping to get away from London to forget the bitterness in work & I think the next lot of poems will be sweeter and more happy.'* An article he wrote in May 1921 seemed to say more about his own dilemma than that of others: 'How can poetry, which is essentially order, affirmation, achievement, be created in an age, a *milieu*, of profound doubt and discouragement?'* In his review of *Exile and Other Poems* for the *Times Literary Supplement* Edmund Blunden wrote: 'War experience interferes with [Mr Aldington's] present experience like a noonday spectre. Where it does not manifest itself in actual images we are conscious of it as an anger and bitterness of aspect. It seems to lead Mr Aldington into gestures of disgust which do not belong to the poet in him.'*

Part I: 'Exile'

Some of the poems in the first section had been written – and appeared in journals – as early as 1919, and we can trace the development of feeling as well as observing the continuities.* In the early poems, the memories are vivid and haunting, the images of death graphic, even Gothic; in 'Eumenides' the survivor guilt he had expressed in 'In a Palace Garden' has been transformed into the notion of the 'murdered self', the chilling perception that it is his own 'self which had its passion for beauty' that has died. The intense preoccupation with mortality that his war experience has given him is particularly apparent in the early poems such as 'Bones' and 'Meditation', as is the sense that this unwelcome but profound knowledge has set him apart: he is 'Le Maudit', the cursed, 'stand[ing] alone in the darkness / Awaiting the tardy finish.' In 'Bones', 'Having Seen Men Killed' and 'Truth' the poet attempts to disengage himself from his morbid preoccupation with death through the use of humour, while the later poems stress the efforts he has made to regain health and wholeness by seeking a quiet environment in a rural setting, through reading, work and, particularly, through contact with nature. Literature might even, through the 'companionship of the immemorial dead', soften the intensity of his consciousness of mortality, but in 'Truth' books have become 'cursed croaking sirens / Written by old men moping at their aches', and in 'At a Gate by the

Way' the poet's 'aching eyes' are 'hot [...] with scanning many books' and his brain 'dry with thoughts of many men'. 'Freedom' suggests that nature – and its associations with the Hellenic world he had always loved – has brought him 'through hate and pity, / Desire and anguish' to release; however, the use of the word 'indifference' suggests something else – a *suppression* of the emotions rather than a deliverance from them.* In 'At a Gate by the Way', clearly written in Aldington's Padworth days and almost certainly addressed to F.S. Flint, though the ghosts and nightmares no longer stalk him, the scene before him prompts the realisation: 'So poor my harvest to this golden wealth, / So teased my spirit to this opulent peace.'

The contrast between civilisation and materialism, often cast as Hellenism and modernity, that featured in Aldington's pre-war poetry persists in 'Exile' and 'Rhapsody in a Third-Class Carriage', while he continues to employ groups of related adjectives to create mood and tone, here principally words suggestive of coldness and aloofness, often associated with space and the stars ('the immense sky, naked and starry', 'fields crisp with new frost', 'the cold sterile wind from colourless space', 'the brief shrill clang of ice on glass') and ones conveying a sense of tranquillity ('peace of the slowly rising tranquil moon', 'shadowy windless places / Where sea moss fringes quiet pebbles', 'the calm lamplight'), detachment and peace of mind being the qualities for which he longs.

In his post-war poetry Aldington adhered for the most part to the free-verse forms he had always used and which were an essential feature of Imagism. In *Exile and Other Poems* form is adjusted according to the voice and tone of the individual poem. In the most personal, intimate and reflective poems such as 'Meditation' and 'In the Palace Garden' he employs a loosely paragraphed free-verse form; the exception is 'At a Gate by the Way', where the paragraphs are primarily in blank verse, a form in better keeping with the more subdued tone of his self-questioning here. However, Aldington also has a more rhetorical style – one which he had begun to employ in some of his wartime verse. These poems are characterised by all or some of the following features: classical allusions, a stylised and discursive plural speaking voice reminiscent of the Greek tragic chorus, insistent rhetorical questions, the mode of a prayer or an apostrophe, a declamatory tone or one of exhortation. 'Exile', 'Le Maudit', 'Rhapsody in a Third-Class Carriage', 'Retreat', 'Nightingale', 'Papillons' and 'Truth' all exhibit some of these characteristics. These poems, while ostensibly in free verse, tend towards the accentual, even at times – as in 'Exile' – towards the metric. Of course, there are poems that partake of both the 'realist' and the more formal and stylised features – 'Freedom' and 'Eumenides', for example. That Aldington was at ease with metric forms is clearly exhibited in the 'Words for Music' section of the collection, but also in the poems here that employ humour – 'Bones' and 'To Those who Played for Safety in Life' – and in his translation of Villon, 'Epitaph in Ballade Form'.

Part II: 'Words for Music'

This section consists of ten (numbered) 'Songs for Puritans', five (titled) 'Songs for Sensualists' and two longer poems, described as 'metrical exercises'.

The 'Songs for Puritans' are, as the title suggests, poems to provoke puritan sensibilities, earthy and even bawdy in tone and employing innuendo. The 'Songs for Sensualists', on the other hand, are an admonition to libertines, adopting a more rarefied approach to love and beauty. Both groups are conscious imitations of the lyric poetry of the 'Cavalier' poets such as Robert Herrick (1591–1674), Thomas Carew (1594–1640), Richard Lovelace (1618–57) and John Suckling (1609–42). Aldington adopts their style – short metrically regular lyrics, usually iambic tetrameters in rhymed couplets or quatrains – and their characteristic tone, subjects and themes. Their models were classical Latin poets and their poetry celebrated female beauty, love and sex with wit and humour, showing a consciousness of mortality and a consequent philosophy which has been called *carpe diem*. This phrase comes from the injunction of the Roman poet Horace '*Carpe diem, quam minimum credula postero*' ('pluck the day, trusting as little as possible in the next one'), the final words of *Odes* 1.11, one of many poems Horace addressed to idealised women. This notion is expressed in the opening lines of Herrick's 'To the Virgins, to Make Much of Time':

> Gather ye rosebuds while ye may,
> Old time is still a-flying;
> And this same flower that smiles today
> Tomorrow will be dying.

Aldington echoes this idea in poem 'VI', which begins '*Pulvis et umbra*' ('We are but dust and shadow'), a further quotation from Horace, and goes on to remind his reluctant lover that 'we are borne to lie / Loveless and chilly in th'uncomely tomb'.

INTRODUCTION

Like the lyrics of the Cavalier poets and their Latin models, many of these poems address the lover directly. Herrick's 'Bid Me to Live' was a favourite of H.D. and Aldington and used by H.D. for the title of her *roman à clé* about their relationship. It ends:

> Thou art my life, my love, my heart,
> The very eyes of me;
> And hast command of every part,
> To live and die for thee.

Aldington's use of stylised Greek names for the women in his poems and the poetic convention of direct address to the beloved is imitative both of the Cavaliers and of their models in Latin love elegy, which included Catullus, Ovid and Propertius as well as Horace. Another important influence was neo-Latin Renaissance poetry, itself largely modelled on classical Latin lyric. Aldington was very familiar with this body of poetry, and published several translations from it. The 'Songs for Puritans' and 'Songs for Sensualists' combine elements from all of these models, along with echoes of Shakespeare, into deceptively simple-seeming lyrics that are in fact the fruit of deep erudition.

Aldington wrote in the introduction to the second edition of his *Collected Poems 1915–1923* that the two poems described as 'Metrical Exercises' arose 'partly from the conviction that I needed to steep myself in English poetry again after so long an exile […] and partly from the fact that short poems were no longer adequate to express what I wanted to say.'* He would indeed concentrate almost exclusively in subsequent years on longer poems, publishing five such works between

1924 and 1938. His models for 'The Berkshire Kennet' and 'A Winter Night' were, he tells us, Edmund Waller (1606–87) and Andrew Marvell (1621–78). Though stylised pastiches in the pastoral tradition, the two poems do not lack gravitas, echoing the personal themes that occur in the poems of Section One, the healing powers of nature, literature and a quiet life. The tone, however, contrasts with that of poems such as 'Eumenides' and 'At a Gate by the Way', suggesting that even with the solace of nature and rural solitude, Aldington found achieving health of spirit an arduous and ongoing struggle.

ELIZABETH VANDIVER AND
VIVIEN WHELPTON, 2023

---

7   *a man's capacity... himself*: Ben Shephard, *A War of Nerves: Soldiers and Psychiatrists 1914–1994* (London: Pimlico, 2002), p. xviii.

10 *At dawn one morning... civilised men*: *Death of a Hero* (London: Penguin Books, 2014), p. 335.

11 *What you say... mediocre critic*: Richard Aldington to F.S. Flint, 17th May 1919 (Letter no. 159 in Michael Copp, *Imagist Dialogues: Letters between Aldington, Flint and Others* (Cambridge: Lutterworth Press, 2009)).

11 *Two days ago... my true fate*: The poem 'In the Palace Garden' was written in response to this experience.

12 *I wonder if you realise... have not*: Richard Aldington to Clement Shorter, 17th March 2019 (Leeds).

12 *I don't expect... I get cold*: Richard Aldington to Amy Lowell, 31st March 1919 (Harvard).

12 *I had to go away... deferred shellshock*: Richard Aldington to Amy Lowell, 11th October 1919 (Harvard).

12 *In December 1919... reviewing*: Aldington first lived in the hamlet of Hermitage, but moved to the village of Padworth in December 1920.

INTRODUCTION

13   *when the whole of Europe... disorder and neglect*: 'Letter from London', *Poetry*, 15.4 (January 1920), pp. 226–227.

13   *[N]o rumble... barbed wire*: *Life for Life's Sake: A Book of Reminiscences* (New York: Viking Press, 1941), p. 239.

13   *With the end of the war... antipathies*: *Life for Life's Sake*, p. 216.

14   *No doubt... more happy*: Richard Aldington to Harriet Monroe, 15th October 1919 (Chicago). Monroe did not publish the poems he enclosed.

14   *How can poetry... doubt and discouragement?*: 'The Poet and Modern Life', *Poetry*, 18.2 (May 1921), p. 99.

15   *War experience... poet in him*: Edmund Blunden, *Times Literary Supplement* (6th December 1923).

15   *Some of the poems... observing the continuities*: The journal record is as follows:

    'Freedom', July 1919 (*Monthly Chapbook*, 1.1, p. 31).
    'Bones', December 1919 (*Coterie*, 3, p. 26).
    'In the Palace Garden', February 1920 (*To-Day*, 6.36, p. 216).
    'Le Maudit', April 1920 (*Coterie*, 4, p. 14).
    'Papillons', July 1920 (*To-Day*, 7.41, p. 182).
    'Nightingale', July 1922 (*Double Dealer*, 4.19, p. 7).
    'Six Songs for Puritans', August 1922 (*Dial*, 73, pp. 191–93).
    'Having Seen Men Killed' and 'Rhapsody in a Third-Class Carriage', March 1923 (*Monthly Chapbook*, 2.35, pp. 8–9).
    'The Berkshire Kennet', September 1923 (*To-Day*, 10.55, pp. 27–29) and October 1923 (*The Yale Review* 13.1, pp. 81–84).
    'Exile' October 1923 (*Dial*, 75, pp. 323–24).

Additionally, a letter from Richard Aldington to Harriet Monroe dated the 2nd of August 1920 (Chicago) refers to Monroe's rejection of 'Eumenides' for inclusion in *Poetry*, allowing us to date that poem.

16   *'Freedom' suggests... from them*: The early date of 'Freedom' – July 1919 – suggests in any case that this sense of achievement was premature.

19   *partly... I wanted to say*: *Collected Poems 1915–1923*, 2nd edn (London: Allen and Unwin, 1933), p. xii.

EXILE

AND OTHER POEMS

I
EXILE

EXILE

'Do you dwell on the snowy promontory of Mimas?'

How shall we utter
This horror, this rage, this despair?
How shall we strike at baseness,
Cut through disgust with scorn?
How rend with slashed fingers
The bars and walls of the lives
Which blacken the air and pure light?

What are they? Alien, brutish,
Base seed of Earth's ravished womb.
Shall we yield our light and our truth –
The flash of the helm,
And the foam-grey eyes and the hair
Braided with gold,
Steel mail on a firm breast?
Shall we yield?

Their life, their truth?
O laugh of disdain!
If ours be a goddess

Chaste, proud and remote,
What is theirs?
A boastful woman, a whore,
One greasy of flesh, stale
With hot musty perfume —
While ours —
Firm-fleshed as the treeless hills,
With her rigid breasts and hard thighs,
Cold and perfect and fresh —
Fields crisp with new frost —
Sets the violet-crown in her hair,
Turns an unstained brow to the sky.

Let us stand by the earth-shaking sea
Unfurrowed by a hull,
Let us move among beeches and oaks
Unprofaned by loud speech;
Let us reverence the sacred earth
And the roar of unbridled falls
And the crash of an untamed sea.
Let us shade our eyes from the sun
And gaze through the leaves,
Far, most far —
Shall we see her hill
And the marble front of her house
And herself, standing calm,
Many-coloured, triumphant, austere?

EUMENIDES

IT is at night one thinks,
At night, staring with sleepless eyes
At the narrow moonlit room.
Outside the owls hoot briefly,
And there are stars
Whose immortal order makes one shudder.

I do not need the ticking of my watch
To tell me I am mortal;
I have lived with, fed upon death
As happier generations feed on life;
My very mind seems gangrened.

What am I, lying here so still,
Staring till I almost see the silence?
What am I?
What obscure fragment of will?
What paltry life cell?

Have I not striven and striven for health?
Lived calmly (as it seemed) these many months,
Walked daily among neat hedged fields,
Watched the long pageant of the clouds,

Loved, drawn into my being, flowers,
English flowers – the thin anemones,
The honey drops of tufted primroses,
Wild scented hyacinths, white stitchwort,
The spotted orchis, tall scentless violets,
Larch buds, green and scarlet,
Noted the springing green
Of white ash, birch and heavy oak,
Lived with the noblest books, the noblest friends,
Looked gay, laughed free, worked long?

I have done all this,
And yet there are always nights
I lie awake staring with sleepless eyes,
And what is my mind's sickness,
What the agony I struggle with,
I can hardly tell.

Loos, that horrible night in Hart's Crater,
The damp cellars of Maroc,
The frozen ghostly streets of Vermelles,
That first night-long gas bombardment –
O the thousand images I see
And struggle with and cannot kill –
That boot I kicked
(It had a mouldy foot in it)
The night K.'s head was smashed
Like a rotten pear by a mortar,
The other night I trod on the dead man
And all the officers were hit…

These, like Eumenides, glide about me,
Fearful memories of despair and misery,
Tortured flesh, caked blood, endurance,
Men, men, and the roar of shells,
The hissing lights, red, green, yellow,
The clammy mud, the tortuous wire,
The slippery boards...

It is all so stale,
It has been said a thousand times;
Millions have seen it, been it, as I;
Millions may be haunted by these spirits
As I am haunted;
May feel, as I feel, in the darkness,
Their flesh dripping into corruption,
Their youth and love and gaiety
Dissolved, violently slain, annihilated.

What is it I agonise for?
The dead? They are quiet;
They can have no complaint.
No, it is my own murdered self –
A self which had its passion for beauty,
Some moment's touch with immortality –
Violently slain, which rises up like a ghost
To torment my nights,
To pain me.
It is myself that is the Eumenides,
That will not be appeased, about my bed;
It is the wrong that has been done me
Which none has atoned for, none repented of,
Which rises before me, demanding atonement.

Tell me, what answer shall I give my murdered self?

LE MAUDIT

Women's tears are but water;
The tears of men are blood.

He sits alone in the firelight
And on either side drifts by
Sleep, like a torrent whirling,
Profound, wrinkled and dumb.

Circuitously, stealthily,
Dawn occupies the city;
As if the seasons knew of his grief,
Spring has suddenly changed into snow.

Disaster and sorrow
Have made him their pet;
He cannot escape their accursed embraces.
For all his dodgings
Memory will lacerate him.

What good does it do to wander
Night hours through city streets?
Only that in poor places

LE MAUDIT

He can be with common men
And receive their unspoken
Instinctive sympathy.
What has life done for him?
He stands alone in the darkness
Like a sentry never relieved,
Looking over a barren space,
Awaiting the tardy finish.

BONES

Now when this coloured curious web
    Which hides my awkward bones from sight
Unrolls, and when the thing that's I –
A pinch of lighted dust that flashes –
Has somehow suddenly gone out,
What quaint adventures may there be
For my unneeded skeleton?

Some men's bones are left (like trees
Which cannot move from where they root)
On open hills or low damp hollows,
Wherever war has struck them down;
And some bones after many years
A waggish bomb digs up, and strews –
Thighbones and ribs mixed up with coffins –
About a well bombarded town;
And some are plunged with ancient wreckage
Where fishes with blue bulging eyes
Slide past, and clouds of tiniest shells
In ages make a rocky cover;
And some lie here and some lie there

BONES

Until they moulder quite away,
Some in the village garth and some
In quiet suburban labelled rows,
And some are powdered up in fire
And some are shown in dull museums…

Now, while his flesh remains, a man
Is something; but who feels akin
To any nameless poor old bones?
Even she, who with miraculous lips
Set little flowering plots of kisses
Over our body, will not care
To hug us when our bones are dry;
And she who carried us nine months
And built them with her vital blood
Might pass them by and never know
These were the bones so hard to bear;
And, likelier still, our dearest child
Would scorn to know us so unveiled,
Unwilling to believe his flesh,
Still firm and petal-sweet, was bred
By such a pitiful old wreck.

But, in the end, the bones go too,
And drift about as dust which hangs
In a long sun-shaft, or dissolve
Into the air to help build up
The pulpy tissues of fine leaves
Or heavier flakes of ruddy flesh,
Or even someone else's bones.

I leave to those superior minds
Who make theology their care
The task of settling whose shall be
These much-used frameworks at the last;
I rather see a wearier world
Shed, aeons hence, its comely flesh
To dance, a mournful skeleton,
Sedately round a dingier sun.

MEDITATION

As I sit here alone in the calm lamplight,
Watching the red embers
Slowly fade and crumble into grey dust,
With that impenetrable silence
Of long night about me
And the companionship of the immemorial dead
At hand upon my shelves,
Then, when I have freed myself
From trivial designs and false longings,
When I have fortified my soul
To endure the rough shock of truth,
Then I can think without trembling or whimpering
That I must see you dead,
That I must press down your useless eyelids,
Extend your arms, smooth down your hair,
And set upon your lips a withered flower,
The poor last kiss.

In the imagination
I have endured all that without a tear;
Yet, if it were not that above all things
I seek and cling to my own truth,

I would cozen my agony with any lie,
Any far-fetched similitude, any dream
Which would lighten with hope this heavy certitude;
I would kiss the feet of man or woman
Who would prove to me your immortality,
Prove to me your new life circles this life
As the immense sky, naked and starry,
Circles with its illimitable round
The low white roof of our cottage.

Yet, as I would not catch your love with a lie,
But force you to love me as I am,
Faulty, imperfect, human,
So I would not cheat your inward being
With untrue hopes nor confuse pure truth with a legend.
This only I have:
I am true to my truth, I have not faltered;
And my own end, the sudden departure
From the virile earth I love so eagerly,
Once such a sombre matter, now appears nothing
Beside this weightier, more torturing bereavement.

IN THE PALACE GARDEN

THE yews became a part of me,
The long walks edged with sparse flowers,
The fluttering green fringes of elm leaves
Blurring the washed blue sky,
The long shivering ripples of the river,
Bird-calls, all we saw and did,
Became me, built me up,
Helped me to love you.
I was happy.
It was enough not to be dead,
Not to be a black spongy mass of decay
Half-buried on the edge of a trench,
More than enough to be young and gay,
To know my lips were such
Yours would be glad to meet them.
I loved you with my old miseries
Which were no longer miseries,
With the scent of the lilacs
And the softly sprinkling fountain,
And the kind glances of passers.
How did it happen then?
The sun did not cease shining,

The water rippled just as fleetly,
I loved you just as indiscreetly –
But gradually my golden mood tarnished,
Happiness hissed into nothing –
Metal under a fierce acid –
And I was whispering:
'This happiness is not yours;
It is stolen from other men.
Coward! You have shirked your fate.'

EPITAPH IN BALLADE FORM

WHICH VILLON MADE FOR HIMSELF AND HIS FRIENDS,
WAITING TO BE HANGED WITH THEM

Brothers among men who after us shall live,
Let not your hearts' disdain against us rise,
For if some pity for our woe ye have,
The sooner God your pardon shall devise.
Behold, here five or six of us we peise;
As to our flesh, which we fed wantonly,
Rotten, devoured, it hangeth mournfully;
And we, the bones, to dust and ash are riven,
Let none make scorn of our infirmity,
But pray to God that all we be forgiven.

If, brothers, we cry out, ye should not give
Disdain for answer, even if justice 'tis
That murders us. This thing ye should believe,
That always all men are not wholly wise;
Pray often for us then, not once or twice,
Before the fair son of the Virgin Mary,
Lest that – for us – his grace prove injury
And we beneath the lord of hell be driven.

Now we are dead, cease importunity
And pray to God that all we be forgiven.

The rain doth weaken all our strength and lave
Us, the sun blackens us again and dries;
Our eyes the ravens hollow like a grave;
Our beards and eyebrows are plucked off by pies.
Never rest comes to us in any wise;
Now here, now there, as the wind sways, sway we,
Swung at the wind's high pleasure ceaselessly,
More pecked by birds than hazelnuts that ripen.
Be ye not then of our fraternity,
But pray to God that all we be forgiven.

ENVOI

Prince Jesus, above all hast mastery,
Let not high hell become our seigneury;
There we have nought to do nor order even.
Brothers, keep here no thought of mockery,
But pray to God that all we be forgiven.

AT A GATE BY THE WAY

S TAND here a moment, friend,
And look across the silent garnered fields;
See how they turn like huge-limbed country gods,
Their labour ended, to a solemn rest —
A rest so like to death that if they think
Their thoughts are those that are befitting death.
With them is peace,
Peace of bland misty skies and hushed winds
Steadily whispering comfort above them,
Peace of the slowly-rising tranquil moon,
Peace of the sombre woods whose leaves,
Heavily drooping, pine but fall not yet;
Peace that the fruit is plucked, the wheatstalks shorn,
And entered all the increase of the year,
Peace, humble but august.

Would you not joy to share in such a mood,
The long task fitly ended, peace at heart,
Under such skies, at such an hour as this?

O friend, why is it that the fields have peace
And we have none? I press my hands
Softly against my aching eyes and feel

How hot they are with scanning many books;
My brain is dry with thoughts of many men,
My heart is faint with deaths of many gods.
I know I live only because I suffer.
I know of truth only because I seek,
Only because I need it know I love.

Hunters of truth and wisdom!
O friend, who sped that bitter speech?
What soft-tongued foe whispered that dear deceit?
We have hunted, you and I, these many years;
Either the game is scant, the luck is thwart,
Or we are mole-eyed or the gods are cruel,
For what we seized breathless with joy
Turned rotten in our hands and what we missed
Seemed ever the one quarry that we sought.

No need to answer. I know, I know
All you would say; I know our search
Is nobler than the common tumult;
We are nearer the gods than those who run and fly.
The shadows we pursue may not be shadows,
The dreams we live with may be more than dreams…
All this I hope; but when the autumn comes
And heavy carts sway loaded to the barns,
And swallows gather to be gone and rooks
Flock to the fields for scattered grain,
O friend, I am filled with musing and distrust,
So poor my harvest to this golden wealth,
So teased my spirit to this opulent peace.

Come, what were you saying of Lucretius?

RHAPSODY IN A THIRD-CLASS CARRIAGE

DEADNESS of English winter, dreariness,
cold sky over provincial towns, mist.
Melancholy of undulating trams
solitary jangling through muddy streets,
narrowness, imperfection, dullness,
black extinguisher over English towns;
mediocre women in dull clothes –
their nudity a disaster –
heavy cunning men (guts and passbooks),
relics of gentry, workmen on bicycles,
puffy small whores, baby carriages,
shops, newspapers, bets, cinemas, allotments…

These are your blood; their begetters
made in the same bed as yours
(horror of copulation),
colossal promiscuity of flesh through centuries
(seed and cemeteries).
Sculptor! show Mars
bloody in gas-lit abattoirs,

Apollo organist of Saint Mary's,
Venus of High Street, Athena,
worshipped at National schools.
Painter! there are beets in allotments,
embankments, coal-yards, villas, grease,
interpret the music orchestra,
trams, trains, cars, hobnails, factories –
O poet! chant them to the pianola,
to the metronome in faultless verse…

FREEDOM

At last, after years, I am saturated
With pity and agony and tears;
At last I have reached indifference;
Now I am almost free –
A gold pellet of sunlight
Dropped, curdling, into green water.

The grass, which is one with our flesh
And bends like an old man
Back to the mould, their mother,
Beckons with long fingers
The poplar nymphs and white ash dryads
To caress their white feet dancing,
Weightless, pale and immortal.

The dead may be myriad,
But my nostrils are sweet with crushed leaves,
My eyes clear as flowers,
My hands stainless;
About me is opulent light
That drenches the lightless sea,
Piercing shadowy windless places
Where sea-moss fringes quiet pebbles.

Over harsh slopes the centaurs gallop
With whistling manes, a rattle of hoofs;
White shapes rustle the dew-dripping thickets
Slim fauns dance by the grass track.
I have passed through hate and pity,
Desire and anguish, to this:
I am myself,
I am free.

RETREAT

Let there be silence sometimes,
A space of starless night –
A silence, a space of forgetfulness
Away from seething of lives,
The rage of struggle.

Let there be a time of retreat,
A hiding of the sun and all colours,
For the soul to ride at ease in darkness;
For the coldness of no-life
To soothe life's burning.

Let there be rest
For wearied eyes to ease their labour
And wander across great distances,
For the spirit to slip the chain of hours
And drift in Atlantic waves of time.

Grant peace;
For a space let there be no roar
Of wheels and voices, no din
Of steel and stone and fire.

Let us cleanse ourselves from the sweat and dirt,
Let us be hushed, let us breathe
The cold sterile wind from colourless space.

HAVING SEEN MEN KILLED...

WHEN by chance
　　As I turn up the brow of the hill,
At a glance
I perceive there's a new grave to fill,
And I see all the poor apparatus of death –

The straight hole
And the planks and the lowering rope;
And the toll
Of the bell and the mirage of hope
In the words
Duly mumbled for those that remain –

Then I smile
'Fine morning,' nod to the sexton's nod,
For a while
Wonder if Einstein proves or disproves God,
But how soon
Find myself cheerfully humming a tune.

NIGHTINGALE

Night winds beat my naked flesh,
Waves of air rush over me.
The young moon stands among frozen clouds;
Far off as death burn the ice-sparkles which are stars.
A wall of rough black pine
Cuts the pale sky.

Your voice –
Ah, chastest, coldest thing!
The brief shrill clang of ice on glass,
The note of fragile metal sharply struck,
The lapse of waters.
Ah, virginal delight!
The woods hold you
And the boughs frozen with dew.

This is no love-song,
No breath of wine and summer flowers,
No murmur of desire;
But such a hymn,
Fierce, lonely and untamed,
As the Troezenian hunter sang
Before the marble shrine.

NIGHTINGALE

So wild a song once rose
From the women of Artemis
In some cold hidden valley
Where trees sombrely ringed
A black lake and cold mist glided
As the first moonrays
Glittered through clouds.

These foam-frail girls
Greek sailors saw beyond their prows,
Whose flesh was cooled by the waves' heart,
Whose veins ran spray of the storm,
Sang this song
As dawn stood grey on the sea's rim.

But this is no love-song,
No echo of kisses.

PAPILLONS

(*BALLET RUSSE*)

What phantasm of the heart of men
So whitely and so wanly
Gibes at us?

Fool!
Had your heart the warmth
That burns in the thin candle-heart,
You had not lost her.

White —
As one who trembles at her gold scorn —
You ask for treachery.

Be red, be blood-red, brother,
And she'll not dare
To dance to other colder lips than yours!

TRUTH

TRUTH! if my words grow wan and cold
   The fault is yours.
Yet what a fool was I,
Like the farm zany in the nursery tale,
To barter a full bag of coined fancies
For your lean script of verities.
What a mouldy cheat was this!
Truth, I suspect your dwelling-place
Is round about old graves and wormy tombs
Inscribed '*Cras tibi, hodie mihi*';
I never met you at a kindly feast
Or with a friend before a blazing fire
Or walking in the sunshine as I sang.
But books, books – cursed croaking sirens –
Written by old men moping at their aches,
Or young men skilled in acids and despair,
Vaunted you, described you,
Offered to impart you for a fee.

There are fools and fools.
Gay fools whose hours pass merrily
And solemn, nasty fools

Whose dismal witchcraft
Makes pigsties of our marriage-beds,
    Schedules the spring,
    Cuts flowers in zinc,
    Turns wine to ink,
    Lops poor Puck's wing.

O Satan! You've disguised yourself as Truth
And made a solemn fool of more than me;
But by these presents, firmly weighed and penned,
I here renounce you and your verminous tricks.

Come, happy Falsehood,
Once again,
Make me a merry fool.

TO THOSE WHO PLAYED FOR SAFETY IN LIFE

I also might have worn starched cuffs,
Have gulped my morning meal in haste,
Have clothed myself in dismal stuffs
Which prove a sober City taste;

I also might have rocked and craned
In undergrounds for daily news,
And watched my soul grow slowly stained
To middle-class unsightly hues...

I might have earned ten pounds a week!

I I

WORDS FOR MUSIC

'Od's-life! must one swear to the truth of a song?'

PRIOR

SONGS FOR PURITANS

I

SUFFER my too ambitious hand
   To range these low delicious hills,
Invest me freedman of a land
   Exile from which dejects and kills;
With pious lips let me revere
The sacred roses cherished there.

I'll gather no more garlands now –
   Mere bubbles of imperfect light –
Since in that secret country grow
   Petals so delicate and light.
And when for love of flowers I pine,
My senses shall exult o'er thine.

II

Unlike that aged Teian boaster
    And those who ape his senile lies,
I cannot show a monstrous roster
    Of ladies captive to my eyes.

Yet five or six I might discover
    (Did grateful prudence not restrain)
Who felt a pleasure-giving lover
    Should not be cut, but come again.

If this were ill, may they forgive me;
    They never seemed to take alarm;
Whate'er John Wesley says, believe me,
    Women know best what does them harm.

III

EUPHEMIA studies law, Aminta
    Inspects the ailments of the poor,
Eudocia prays and Araminta
    Numbers the stars on heaven's floor;
Yet Chloe for my mistress I decree,
Whose only art is artless love of me.

'Tis not the statute binds together,
    Physic ignores the wounds we share,
Love works in dull or starry weather
    And nakedness suits not with prayer;
Then let your learning, Chloe, still consist
In all the various ways of being kist.

IV

BELIEVE not, Chloe, all your grace
Can dwell within that lovely face,
Believe not all your beauty lies
In the mild prison of those eyes.

Yet, Chloe, think not I incline
To passions abstract and divine,
'Tis not a soul alone could move
This ardent flesh to sue for love.

But when that rose-tipped breast I see,
Or the white splendour of your knee,
I covet a more precious fleece
Than ever Jason brought to Greece.

V

WHEN to Dorinda I impart
    My passion,
She vows the mistress of my heart
    Is fashion,
That Celia, Chloe and Lucinda
Shall never rule with proud Dorinda.

I crave more beauties than do stir
    My vision;
For all reply she shows me her
    Derision.
Must I then suffer this, a martyr
That dares not rise above her garter?

If she persists a prude, I swear
    I'll leave her
Till some chaste, clumsy cuckold dare
    Relieve her;
As heavy guns take virgin trenches,
So husbands smooth our way to wenches.

VI

Pulvis et umbra! Chloe, why
   Quench my desire with ill-bred gloom,
Since many an amorous death we die
Ere we are borne to lie
   Loveless and chilly in th'uncomely tomb?

Why, pretty fool, is that a tear
   Wronging the cheek I kissed so late?
There is no dust nor shadow here;
Come, kiss me without fear,
   And let me bring you to the ivory gate.

VII

Daphnis, pray breathe this pastoral vein;
   Strew not my broidered sheets with flowers
      Dripping cold rain;
Can any civil maid embrace
Daffodils dropped in freezing showers
      That soil her lace?
Be (if you choose) a poet, but
Expect to find my window shut;
Though Chloe loves whene'er she can,
She loves no pseudo-shepherd-man.

VIII

CHLOE, the gods are too remote
   From this unruly cloud-wrapped ball,
Too tranquil, as the rose-leaves float
   On wine-cups in th'Olympian hall,
To keep a watch on you and me
And frown at lost virginity.

The rose must shed its fragile flower
   Before the slim red fruit appears,
Unloose your garments like a shower
   Of falling petals, quit your fears,
And suffer my religious hand
To pluck the fruit no eye has scanned.

IX

O reverend sir, cease to upbraid
   A simple man who lives by reason,
Who never tried to thwart your trade
   By dull invectives out of season:

Desist, then, from your dreary labour;
   I know the errors of my life;
But, though I do not love my neighbour,
   How often have I loved his wife!

X

SIR Pious, pray you hide your eyes;
  By all the saints! you shall not look;
For yonder where the sunshine lies
  Chloe is bathing in the brook:

Chloe is bathing in the brook
  And glads a pagan sight like mine;
But you, Sir Pious, con your book
  And learn that pearls are not for swine.

SONGS FOR SENSUALISTS

A SOPHISTRY OF DURATION

TELL me not beauty dies like dew
    The envious sun draws trembling up,
Nor liken hers to that brief hue
    Flushes the rose's tender cup –
For things like her so lovely are
They should outlive the bravest star.

If all my senses still conspire,
    Ere their meridian be past,
To set the blossoms of desire,
    The worm shall not exult at last;
Her children and my words I trust
Shall speak her grace when we are dust.

A GARDEN HOMILY

COME, thrust your hands in the warm earth
   And feel her strength through all your veins,
Breathe her full odours, taste her mirth
   That laughs away imagined pains.
Touch here life's very womb, but know
This substance makes your grave also.

Shrink not; your flesh is no more sweet
   Than flowers which daily blow and die;
Nor are your mien and dress so neat;
   Nor half so pure your lucid eye.
And yet – by flowers and earth I swear
You're neat and pure and sweet and fair.

WORDS FOR MUSIC

Go tell the shepherd's star, when first
   The evening fans her spark awake,
That light is murderous and accurst –
   But say not Delia faith can break.

Tell the wild rose, when tranquil days
   Have charmed a thousand petals wide,
Tomorrow scatters all her praise –
   But say not Delia's kisses lied.

Swear anything that's monstrous, swear
   That truth is a fantastic lie,
Take oath that Delia is not fair –
   But, oh! that she is false, deny.

MADRIGAL

OH, by what right shall I upbraid
        Beauty that will not let me rest?
What charm shall make to fade
        Those cheeks as fragrantly demure as morn
And quench the perfume of her flowering breast?
  All night I waked forlorn,
        I waked forlorn,
Hearkening the lamentation of the rain,
But daylight brought no slumber to my pain,
        no slumber to my pain.

FROM TASSO

DANCE OF AIR SPIRITS

We are those unseen forms that fly
   Hither and thither in the sky,
Our home the eternal crystalline
Wide spaces of the pure serene
Where wandering breezes gently stray
And no sun brings too hot a day
And there is never wintry weather
To chill us as we dance together;
Now fate and heavenly grace have brought us
To the sight of you who sought us,
Down we glided from the air,
Young and blithe and light and fair,
To teach you how aërial sprites
Gambol in the starry nights,
To rouse your dull and mortal ears
With the music of the spheres.

METRICAL EXERCISES

THE BERKSHIRE KENNET

'Amongst his hills and holts, as on his way he makes,
At Reading once arrived, clear Kennet overtakes
His lord, the stately Thames…'

    DRAYTON'S *POLY-OLBION*

TURN from the city's poisoned air
 And dwell with me a little where
The Kennet, gently flowing, speeds
His scent of green and bruiséd reeds
And water-mints that root in mud,
Cordial and faint; or where his flood
Breaks in a low perpetual roar
Beneath the weir, abrupt and hoar
With ragged foam and trembling spray
Whose perfume damps the hottest day
With cool invisible sweet breath.

Old willows, stout, but near their death,
In winter wave their naked boughs
Beside the stream that roughly ploughs

The loose earth from their roots; in spring
Winds lighter than the swallow's wing
Touch their pale fluttering leaves which throw
A green light on the stream below.
The water-meadows, cool and lush,
Fringed with the ragged hawthorn bush,
Bear lonely elms with shaggy stems –
Green petticoats with ruffled hems –
And oaks in distant clumps, as round
As Latin domes, and poplars sound
And tall as Lombard bell-towers, and
Long aspen screens on either hand.

And all the river's way is lined
With broad reeds rustling in the wind,
And flowers that bend as if they gave
Farewells to every passing wave –
Tall meadow-sweet spreads out as stiff
As Queen Anne's pocket-handkerchief;
And amid willow-herb the sprays
Of loosestrife gold or purple blaze;
And August sees the guelder-rose
Hung with her clustered fruit that glows
Robust and crimson, where in June
Gleamed whiter than the ashen moon
The cold and delicate flowers that shine
Upon the thorny eglantine.
And far across the fields and marsh
The peewit clamours shrill and harsh,
Or – out of sight he wings so high –

The snipe falls drumming from the sky,
Or wary redshanks flit and flute
Clear notes to hush their young brood mute.

O solitude, O innocent peace,
Silence, more precious than the Fleece
That Jason and his fellows sought,
Our greatest riches though unbought,
And hard to find and ill to praise
In noisy and mechanic days!
Yet in these humble meadows they
Have cleansed the wounds of war away,
And brought to my long troubled mind
The health that I despaired to find,
And, while their touch erased the pain,
Breathed the old raptures back again
And in their kindness gave to me
Almost that vanished purity.

Here where the osiers barely sigh
Hour upon hour still let me lie,
Where neither cannon roar nor noise
Of heavy wheels my ear annoys,
And there is none my face to scan
Save some incurious countryman;
And in my cool and hushed nook
I read some old and gentle book
Until in thought I lift my eyes
To rest on dappled English skies,
And hear the stream go murmuring by

And watch the bubbling eddies fly
As Kennet's waters glide for ever
To wed the elder, nobler river…

As on the verge of sleep I nod
I see the ancient river god
Lean on his smooth and polished urn;
His hair is twined with rush and fern
And in his beard are waving reeds
And in his hand are lily seeds.
Ever the marble urn expels
Cool water, pure as that which wells
From some untainted northern hill;
Ever his languid hands do spill
The flowers that nod and dip and smile
Along his banks mile upon mile,
Nor ever do his green eyes shun
The glances of his grateful son.

And if I now invoke him here,
What supercilious lip dare sneer,
What heart that never loved the earth
Dare turn my piety to mirth,
And what vile truckler to the crowd
Scorn me, who live remote and proud?
Then, noble river, take my praise
And grant me more such happy days,
Each evening bring untroubled sleep
As your own waters still and deep,
And let my wealth be more or less,
So it suffice for happiness,

And keep in my untroubled life
The kindness of a comely wife,
And let the years I have been lent
Bring me not fame but sweet content,
And when my days run out and I
Must go, then teach me how to die,
To leave my well-loved solitude
For an enduring quietude.

A WINTER NIGHT

Now the calm acres where I lay
Through half a murmurous summer's day,
Nodding in these drowsy meads
To the curtseying of the reeds,
Are drenched and mournful, harsh and wild.
Hostile to his late spoil'd child,
The turbid river seems to sulk
And hoarsely pours his swollen bulk;
Blind with swirling leaves, the year
Dreads the mort-sheet drawing near,
Cowering hides his frosted head
And mourns his April splendours fled.
The pattering rain falls loud and thick,
Quelling the old clock's gentle tick;
The tossing willows hiss and creak
As if long anguish forced them speak
And curse the loud tormenting gale;
And as their branches groan and wail,
The ivy taps the latticed pane;
The wind howls; and it taps again.

'Clap-to the doors, tomorrow pray';
Tonight be given to mirth and play;
Shut out the wind, shut out the cold,
Shut out the world that's mean and old,
Shut out its madness, but admit
Beauty and memory and wit.

What glowing spirits deign to dwell
Here in this narrow low-pitch'd cell,
What stately pleasures I command
With all Eliza's wits at hand!
And how it charms my amorous looks
To see such ranks of noble books –
For some sweet god to ease man's curse
Gave him the gift of choice old verse;
And those whom dull rich men despise
Taste real revenge by growing wise:
Thus even in hell they ease their pain
With Shakespeare, Marlowe and Montaigne.

Then let me sit and entertain
The fancies that invest my brain,
That wheel and flutter hour by hour
Like moths about a campion flower
On heavy dewless nights of May;
And let them poise and wheel and play,
Fan their pattern'd wings, then soar
To the haunts they kept before,
Leaving in my mind and heart
Coloured dust as they depart...

And if I tell these fancies? Then
I should be scorn'd by stupid men;
Too well I know both friends and foes
Ever to let my heart unclose,
Ever to give what I should keep
A secret to myself and Sleep.
What! give again, as I have given,
Things sacred sent to me from heaven?
No! though my outward life be rude
It keeps the grace of solitude;
No wealthy fool, no titled whore
Passes this quiet cottage door,
No noisy flatterer of the mob
Warms by my Spartan chimney hob!
But O you distant gods that dwell
Somewhere in earth or heaven or hell,
Turn for a moment from his betters
To hear a proud poor man of letters:
Grant that by toil which flatters none
I earn my needs, and that toil done,
Grant me to live still undisturbed;
Keep this proud spirit yet uncurbed;
Leave me my books and peace and health
And heavier wits may plod for wealth;
Let me ne'er lose an honest friend
And keep me free until the end.

NOTES

Exile and Other Poems was published by George, Allen and Unwin in a limited edition of 750 copies in November 1923. George Allen and Unwin had previously published Aldington's *Images of War* (1919). The firm would go on to publish his long poem *Fool i' the Forest* (1925) and collections of his critical journalism, entitled *Literary Studies and Reviews* (1924) and *French Studies and Reviews* (1926). They would also publish his *Collected Poems* in 1929, by which time Chatto and Windus had become Aldington's British publishers. It was also published in the United States, in a similarly limited edition, by the Dial Press. In some instances, spelling and punctuation have been silently corrected, and some archaic forms (e.g. 'to-day', 'to-morrow') have been updated, to make the text more appealing to the modern reader.

I: EXILE

Exile

The epigraph is a paraphrase of Socrates' invocation to the cloud goddesses in Aristophanes' comedy *The Clouds*. Socrates summons the goddesses by saying 'Whether you are sitting on the holy snow-covered peaks of Olympus [...] or dwell in the Maeotic lake, or the snowy crag of Mimas, hear our prayer' (lines 270–74). The plot of *The Clouds* focuses on the contrast between old-fashioned culture and learning and the flashy, insincere rhetoric of modern philosophers such as Socrates and the Sophists – a contrast that is echoed in Aldington's poem; in the preface to his *Collected Poems 1915–1923*, Aldington said that the poem 'was intended (in 1919) to express a contrast between brutal Nationalism and an ideal of civilisation and culture' (p. xii).

The poem presents a contrast between two goddesses, 'ours' and 'theirs'; the goddess representing the former ideal is clearly Athena. Aldington identifies her through her standard attributes of helmet, grey eyes and aegis ('mail on a firm breast'). He references her virginity and her pride in her high status among the Olympians. The epithet 'remote' reflects the fact that, with notable exceptions, including Odysseus and his son Telemachus, Athena tended not to favour individual humans with her direct patronage.

Athena was the patron goddess of Athens, where Pheidias' great chryselephantine statue ('herself, standing calm') stood in the Parthenon ('her house') on the Acropolis ('her hill'). Chryselephantine statues were made of ivory and gold, and the facial features and hair would have been painted ('many-coloured'), as were all ancient statues. '[M]any-coloured' also recalls the first word of Sappho's 'Hymn to Aphrodite', *poikilothron* ('of the many-coloured throne'). Aldington was very familiar with this poem. Athena was the goddess of war, and so the patron of Athens' victories in war ('triumphant').

'Sets the violet-crown in her hair': Pindar (*c*.518–*c*.438 BC) referred to Athens as 'city of the violet crown' (Fragment 77).

'earth-shaking sea': 'Earth-shaker' was a standard epithet of Poseidon.

Eumenides

The title establishes the poem's main theme. The Eumenides or Erinyes of Greek myth were the Furies, ancient goddesses who pursued and punished those who had shed kindred blood. They are best known in literature for their association with Orestes, who killed his mother Clytemnestra to avenge her murder of his father Agamemnon. After this matricide, Orestes was pursued by the Furies, who tormented him with physical suffering and with madness. According to Aeschylus' version in *The Oresteia*, Orestes was eventually acquitted of blood-guilt by standing trial in Athens, with Apollo defending him and Pallas Athena acting as final arbiter; at this point the Furies became beneficent guardians of Athens, under the euphemistic name 'Eumenides' – 'the kindly ones'.

Like Orestes, the poem's speaker is 'haunted' by spirits of vengeance – memories – that threaten him with physical torment and with madness ('my mind's sickness'). The parallel goes deeper. Orestes is guilty of a crime (matricide) that was at the same time an absolute duty (vengeance for his murdered father), and Aldington places the war veteran in the same position: to kill an enemy soldier was simultaneously murder and an inexorable duty, and therefore cannot be resolved in the veteran's mind or incorporated into his understanding of his place in society. Unlike *The Oresteia*, the poem contains no hint of any resolution or absolution for the blood-guilty. The kindred blood the speaker has shed is his own, and he is also the avenger; the poem collapses murdered, murderer and spirits of retribution into one unbearable whole and ends with the unanswerable question, 'What answer shall I give my murdered self?'

This sense of a divided self who was simultaneously killer and victim reappears in Aldington's long poem *A Fool i' the Forest* (1924), where the main character is divided into three selves, 'I', the Conjuror (or the intellect) and the fool Mezzetin (or the creative spirit); the Conjuror kills Mezzetin and 'I' kills the Conjuror. Aldington returns to the Eumenides and the story of Orestes to convey the sense of blood-guilt that haunts former soldiers in *Death of a Hero*, where the novel's narrator several times compares all of post-war society to Orestes pursued by the Eumenides:

> The whole world is blood-guilty, cursed like Orestes, and mad, and destroying itself, as if pursued by an infinite legion of Eumenides. Somehow we must atone, somehow we must free ourselves from the curse – the blood-guiltiness. We must find – where? how? – the greater Pallas who will absolve us on some Acropolis of Justice. But meanwhile the dead poison us and those who come after us.*

Like the poem 'Eumenides', however, the novel ultimately finds no such absolution.

'Eumenides' uses form subtly and powerfully to underline the irrevocability of the speaker's guilt. There are lines of perfect iambic pentameter ('I do not need the ticking of my watch'; 'Lived calmly (as it seemed) these many months'; 'Some moment's touch with immortality'), one line of perfect trochaic pentameter ('Millions may be haunted by these spirits'), and many iambic half-lines, so that the overall impression is of somewhat irregular iambic metre. But there are also lines that resist the iambic pull of the whole, adding palpably to the uneasiness and restlessness that characterise the poem's content.

In the central stanza describing the experiences of war, Aldington calls those memories 'the thousand images I see'. For Aldington, the word 'image' cannot be lightly chosen. But here an 'image' – a mouldy foot still in a boot, a head smashed like a rotten pear – is a powerful evocation of horror. The war has transformed an 'image' from the core around which a poem can crystallise into a source of lasting torment to the poet.

Le Maudit

'He stands alone in the darkness / Like a sentry never relieved': the sentry is a common motif in the aftermath poetry of the First World War. See, for example, Siegfried Sassoon's 'War Experience', Edmund Blunden's 'The Watchers' and Robert Graves's 'Retrospect: The Jests of the Clock'. But only for Aldington does he become an 'accursed figure' (literally *'le maudit'*).

Epitaph in Ballade Form

François Villon, whose poetry Aldington admired, was born in Paris in 1431 or 1432. He was condemned to be hanged in 1462, but the sentence was commuted to banishment in January 1463, after which his fate is unknown. The many other translators of his 'Ballade' include Swinburne and Richard Wilbur. Aldington's translation preserves the original's metre and rhyme-scheme with remarkable fidelity.

'Behold, here five or six of us we peise': Aldington uses the now-obsolete verb *peise* in the sense 'to sink or hang down by virtue of having weight'.

The poem at first glance seems somewhat out of place in this collection, given its status as a translation and its use of regular metre and rhyme. However, the theme of the poem, in which dead men guilty of terrible crime cry out to the living for pity, remembrance and prayer, and warn them against becoming 'of our fraternity', fits remarkably well with Aldington's post-war mood, so much so that Adrian Barlow considers it 'the central statement of this whole sequence of poems.'* As in 'Eumenides', the soldier is simultaneously an offender against society and its victim. 'Like the robber who suffers the ultimate censure of society, the soldier who has survived the war also becomes a scapegoat for society (hence – "exile") and, confessing his guilt, has to face society's ultimate sanction.'* In particular, Villon's description of the ghastly fate of the hanged men's unburied bodies resembles the descriptions in Aldington's 'Bones' of the condition of various buried and unburied bodies. Villon's hanged men, recognising their own crimes in their plea 'even if justice 'tis / That murders us', form a kind of mirror image of the speaker of 'Eumenides', who mourns for his 'violently slain' self.

At a Gate by the Way

'And swallows gather to be gone' is an echo of Keats's 'To Autumn'. Here, as in Keats's poem, Autumn is a symbol of both plenitude and death.

'Come, what were you saying of Lucretius?': Titus Lucretius Carus (d. mid-50s BC) was the author of *De rerum natura*, a six-book poem on Epicurean physics and ethics. Most relevant here is Lucretius' argument in Book 3 that the soul, no less than the body, is composed of atoms and therefore undergoes dissolution at death, so that there can be no afterlife of any kind. Lucretius further argues that this means it is irrational to fear death, since the state of being dead involves no more suffering than the state of not yet being born; both involve total non-existence of the individual. Aldington knew Lucretius' poem well and quotes its opening invocation to Venus in *Death of a Hero*.

Rhapsody in a Third-Class Carriage

Mars was the Roman god of war; Apollo was associated with music, poetry, harmony and prophecy (as well as, later, the Sun); Venus was the goddess of sexual desire; Athena was the patron goddess of Athens and of war. In each of these cases, Aldington has reduced the ancient deity's role to a bathetic modern caricature.

'to the metronome in faultless verse': this inverts the famous Imagist instruction 'to compose in the sequence of the musical phrase, not in the sequence of a metronome'.*

Freedom

Aldington here uses semi-divine figures from Greek mythology to create his imagined peaceful world. Dryads are the nymphs of trees, centaurs are half-man, half-horse hybrids and fauns (satyrs in Greek) are usually depicted as hybrids of man and goat. In ancient myth, centaurs and fauns are wild and unruly creatures, given to sexual violence and excess, but in Aldington's personal mythology they are emblems of rural tranquillity, pre-Christian simplicity and shame-free eroticism. Both Aldington and

H.D. used 'faun' as a name to refer to Aldington himself in their private letters and 'dryad' to refer to H.D.

'The grass, which is one with our flesh' inverts the Biblical 'All flesh is grass' (Isaiah 40:6).

'My nostrils are sweet with crushed leaves' is another echo of Keats, this time 'Ode to A Nightingale'.

Having Seen Men Killed

After attending his father's funeral Aldington wrote to F.S. Flint on the 3rd of May 1921, 'For me the dead are yellow faces, pools of blood, muddy khaki, hurried burials under shellfire [...] I became addicted to wholesale death; so retail death, although it touches me closely, cannot move me greatly.* The poem may well have been written at the time although its first publication was not until March 1923. Like 'Bones', it exhibits a macabre humour but, rather than the stylised metre of the latter, adopts a colloquial realist manner, resembling that of his wartime poem 'Trench Idyll'.

Nightingale

The poem foregrounds the goddess Artemis throughout, beginning with its reference to 'the young moon' in the third line. Artemis, goddess of the hunt and associated with the moon, was one of three virgin goddesses (along with Athena and Hestia). She was involved with important transitions in women's lives; her usual worshippers included young girls on the cusp of puberty and women in the throes of childbirth, and her arrows brought sudden death to women as her brother Apollo's arrows did to men. The 'Troezenian hunter' refers to Hippolytus, the title character of Euripides' play. Aldington refers to this play frequently in his poems, novels and essays, and even in his personal letters. Hippolytus, the illegitimate son of the Athenian hero Theseus and the Amazon queen Hippolyta, rejected Aphrodite and all forms of sexuality and devoted himself to Artemis. The 'marble shrine' here is a temple of Artemis, and the 'hymn / Fierce, lonely and untamed' recalls Hippolytus' first invocation to Artemis in Euripides' play. This leads Aldington to portray female worshippers of the goddess, in a setting 'where trees sombrely ringed / A black lake', recalling the mythic episode when Artemis punishes the hunter Actaeon for inadvertently spying on her bathing in a lake by turning him into a deer which is then torn apart by Actaeon's own hounds.

In the final stanza, the reference is to the Sirens, goddesses who lay in wait for Greek sailors and lured them, by singing, to their deaths on the rocky coasts.

However, the poem also references Keats's 'Ode to a Nightingale'. For both poets the song of the nightingale is a door to the world of the imagination, but those imaginary worlds, in Keats's case an explicit escape from suffering, are very different. Aldington's nightingale does not 'sing of summer in full-throated ease', but has a voice like 'the brief shrill clang of ice on glass' and, rather than Ruth 'amid the alien corn', the poet thinks of Hippolytus 'before the marble shrine' of Artemis. For both poets the nightingale's song is enchanting, even dangerous, and the image of the Sirens singing 'As dawn stood grey on the sea's rim' is not far removed from Keats's 'perilous seas, in faery lands forlorn'. However, where Keats's images are warm, soft and sensuous, Aldington's are cold, sharp and chaste.

Papillons

Michael Fokine's ballet *Les Papillons* premiered in March 1913 at the Maryinsky Theatre in St Petersburg and was restaged by the Ballets Russes. In the ballet Pierrot encounters a group of young women in a park and imagines they are butterflies. Aldington saw and reviewed a 1919 London performance.*
The poem may well date from that time.

Truth

'*Cras tibi, hodie mihi*': 'Today for me, tomorrow for you.'

In this poem and the next, 'To Those Who Played for Safety in Life', Aldington touches on themes that will be crucial for his long poem *A Fool i' the Forest*. The final line of 'Truth' foreshadows the beginning of *Fool*, with the narrator ('I') declaring that he needs to find a fool, a role played in that poem by Mezzetin, a figure from the Commedia dell'Arte. 'To Those Who Played' lays out the ultimate fate of 'I' in *Fool*, as that character becomes an office worker who takes the underground to work each day and is slowly stifled by his humdrum job. The position of these two poems at the end of the first section of *Exile* suggests that the seeds of *Fool i' the Forest* were already germinating in Aldington's mind at this point.

II: WORDS FOR MUSIC

Songs for Puritans

I

The conceit of the female body as geography features in much seventeenth-century love poetry, most famously in John Donne's 'To His Mistress Going to Bed'. Aldington also references Shakespeare here, as 'my too ambitious hand' echoes Romeo's first words to Juliet, 'If I profane with my unworthiest hand / This holy shrine' (*Romeo and Juliet*, Act I, Scene 5).

II

The 'Teian boaster' is the Greek poet Anacreon (*c.*570–478 BC), famed for his erotic verse. Aldington includes quotations and paraphrases from Anacreon in many of his poems.

John Wesley: with his brother Charles, the founder of Methodism.

III

Euphemia, Eudocia and Chloe are all Greek names. 'Chloe' appears in four of Horace's *Odes*. Aminta was the titular hero of a pastoral drama by the Italian poet Torquato Tasso (1544–95). Aldington translates a passage of this play later in this volume, but here treats 'Aminta' as a female name. Araminta was a character in William Congreve's *The Old Bachelor* (1693).

IV

The final couplet refers to the theft of the Golden Fleece from Colchis by Jason and the Argonauts, one of the most famous of Greek myths. Jason was aided in his quest by the Colchian princess Medea, who had fallen in love with him; thus, the mythic theft of the Fleece is associated with an erotic context, which underlines the punning eroticism of Aldington's lines.

V

'Dorinda' appears in John Dryden and William D'Avenant's play *The Enchanted Island* (1667). 'Celia' is Rosalind's cousin in *As You Like It* and was a name also used by Ben Jonson for a character in his play *Volpone*, which includes 'Song: To Celia' (itself a free translation of Catullus 5). 'Lucinda' appears to have been chosen simply to rhyme with 'Dorinda'.

VI

'*Pulvis et umbra*' ('dust and shadow'): Horace *Odes* IV.7 centres on the contrast between the seasons, renewed each year, and human life, cut off by death. It is not a love poem, but Aldington refigures the quoted phrase to recall not only Horace's erotic elegy but also Catullus 5, which exhorts Lesbia to give the poet innumerable kisses since 'when once the brief light fades for us / we must sleep one endless night.'

'Let me bring you to the ivory gate': According to the *Odyssey* (19. 560–9), true dreams come through a Gate of Horn and false dreams through a Gate of Ivory. The best-known occurrence of this idea is in the *Aeneid* (6.893–8), where Aeneas and the Sibyl exit the Underworld through the Gate of Ivory.

VII

The Greek novel *Daphnis and Chloe* (second or third century AD) by Longus is a pastoral romance. The two main characters are both orphans who are brought up by shepherds and who, as they reach their teenage years, fall in love with each other, although they are so completely innocent and uninformed that they do not understand their own emotions and sexual impulses. The novel tells the story of their courtship, tribulations and eventual marriage. It was extremely influential on later European literature.

NOTES

VIII

'Chloe' here is more likely a recollection of Horace than of Longus. Aldington draws on the common Epicurean doctrine of the remote gods, uninterested in human endeavours. The metaphor of a fading or plucked rose for a girl's loss of virginity is extremely common; cf. *Twelfth Night*: 'women are as roses, whose fair flower / Being once displayed, doth fall that very hour' (Act II, Scene 4).

'my religious hand': perhaps another echo of Romeo's 'if I profane with my unworthiest hand'.

Songs for Sensualists

A SOPHISTRY OF DURATION

'Her children and my words I trust / Shall speak her grace when we are dust': the most famous poems expressing the notion that the loved object will survive the grave through their offspring and in the poet's verses are Shakespeare's sonnets, particularly Sonnet 18, which concludes: 'So long as men can breathe or eyes can see, / So long lives this, and this gives life to thee.'

WORDS FOR MUSIC

Delia ('of Delos') is a name for the goddess Artemis, who was born on that island. The Latin elegiac poet Tibullus used Delia as a pseudonym for his mistress, and Samuel Daniel (1562–1619) wrote a cycle of fifty sonnets titled 'Delia'.

'Go tell the shepherd's star' reminds us of the opening of John Donne's 'Song': 'Go and catch a falling star', a poem proclaiming the inconstancy of women, while the lines 'swear / That truth is a fantastic lie' recall Hamlet's letter to

Ophelia: 'Doubt thou the stars are fire, / Doubt that the sun doth move, / Doubt truth to be a liar, / But never doubt I love' (*Hamlet*, Act II, Scene 2).

MADRIGAL

Madrigals were sixteenth and seventeenth-century short polyphonic musical lyrics, with secular texts and elaborate counterpoint. Although this section is titled 'Words for Music', this is the only poem for which Aldington specifies a musical form.* He imitates the madrigal's musical quality and many voices through his lines of differing lengths and the repetition of two phrases as refrains.

FROM TASSO: DANCE OF THE AIR SPIRITS

This is a free translation of the third 'Interlude' in Tasso's pastoral play *Aminta* (1573). The interludes (*intermezzi*) were sung and accompanied by dancing, as Aldington's title indicates. He has simplified the original's complicated rhyme scheme. He greatly admired this play, calling it 'a masterpiece of its genre' in a letter of 1951.*

Metrical Exercises

THE BERKSHIRE KENNET

This poem was also published as a separate booklet in a limited edition of fifty copies (London: Curwen Press, 1923). Malthouse Cottage in Lower Padworth, where Aldington had moved at the end of 1920, was on the Kennet and Avon Canal and just a half-mile walk from the river. In his memoirs Aldington wrote that the Kennet valley had 'the charm of pastoral poetry'.*

NOTES

The *Poly-Olbion* by Michael Drayton (1563–1631) is a lengthy poem of thirty 'songs' in iambic hexameters describing and celebrating the entire country of England and Wales. Each song describes between one and three counties. '*Poly-olbion*' means 'greatly happy' or 'greatly fortunate'.

Marvell's 'The Garden' would seem to have been the likely model both in form and content for this poem, but some of its lines remind us of a more contemporary text, Rupert Brooke's 'The Old Vicarage, Grantchester' (1912), although the latter poem is generally playful in tone.

'more precious than the Fleece / That Jason and his fellows brought': cf. the note on 'Songs for Puritans: IV'. Aldington rarely refers to the myth of the Argonauts; here, the comparison to the Golden Fleece makes 'silence [...] hard to find' the goal of a heroic quest.

'Here where the osiers barely sigh': this whole stanza is particularly reminiscent of Rupert Brooke's 'Grantchester'.

'[T]he elder, nobler river' is the Thames, which the Kennet joins at Reading.

'The ancient river god / Lean on his smooth and polished urn': Aldington's description here follows the standard Roman iconography for a river god, who would be depicted as a mature man, with full beard, reclining by a body of water and leaning his elbow on an urn from which water flowed. Aldington would have seen many such representations of river gods in his travels in Italy, including two famous examples in the Capitoline Museum in Rome.

'Let my wealth be more or less [...] not fame, but sweet content': this wish for a moderate life echoes Solon's description to Croesus of the life of the most fortunate (*olbios*, as in *poly-olbion*) man, Tellus the Athenian, in Herodotus Book 1, although Aldington tellingly omits Solon's inclusion of children and death in battle defending one's country as hallmarks of the truly fortunate man. Aldington greatly admired Herodotus' work.

A WINTER NIGHT

The contrast between the winter weather outside and the warm, welcoming seat by the fire where the speaker can read 'choice old verse' is reminiscent of 'Winter', a Latin poem by Andrea Fracastoro (1476–1553). Aldington's *Latin Poems of the Renaissance* included a translation of this poem.*

'clap-to the doors, to-morrow pray': from *Henry IV, Part I*, where Falstaff says 'Mistress, clap to the doors. Watch tonight, pray tomorrow' (Act II, Scene 4).

'all Eliza's wits at hand': Eliza is Elizabeth I.

'The grace of solitude': Fracastoro's poem is addressed to a friend, to whom the speaker will read Virgil's works. Aldington alters his model here to stress solitude, although the final couplet of his poem does suggest the possibility of an 'honest friend'.

---

88 *The whole world… come after us*: *Death of a Hero* (London: Penguin Books, 2014), p. 24.

90 *the central statement… poems*: Adrian Barlow, *Answers for My Murdered Self* (Francestown, NH: Typographeum, 1987), p. 18.

90 *Like the robber… ultimate sanction*: ibid., p. 18.

91 *to compose… metronome*: F.S. Flint, 'Imagisme', *Poetry: A Magazine of Verse*, 1.8 (March 1913), p. 199.

NOTES

92 *For me the dead... greatly*: Letter no. 209 in Michael Copp, *Imagist Dialogues: Letters between Aldington, Flint and Others* (Cambridge: Lutterworth Press, 2009).

94 *Aldington... London performance*: 'The Russian Ballet', *Sphere* 78 (16th August 1919), p. 160.

98 *the only poem... musical form*: 'Madrigal' was in fact set to music in 1930 by Henry Crowder; Norman T. Gates, ed., *The Poetry of Richard Aldington* (University Park, PA: Pennsylvania State University Press, 1974), p. 118, n. 116.

98 *calling... in a letter of 1951*: Miriam J. Benkovitz, ed., *A Passionate Prodigality: Letters to Alan Bird from Richard Aldington 1949–1962* (NY: New York Public Library, 1975), p. 32.

98 *the charm of pastoral poetry*: *Life for Life's Sake: A Book of Reminiscences* (New York: Viking Press, 1941), p. 246.

100 *Aldington's Latin Poems... this poem*: Richard Aldington, *Latin Poems of the Renaissance*. The Poets' Translation Series. No. 4 (London: Ballantyne, 1915), p. 6. An earlier version of the translation appeared in *New Age* 12.4 (23 November 1912), 25.

MORE CLASSIC POETRY FROM RENARD PRESS

ISBN: 9781804470374
large flapped paperback
£12.99 • 344pp

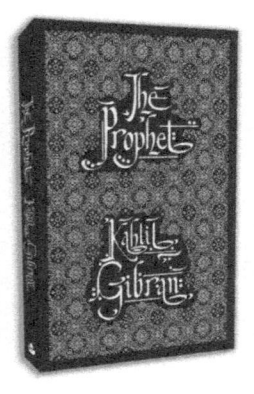

ISBN: 9781913724955
paperback
£6.99 • 112pp

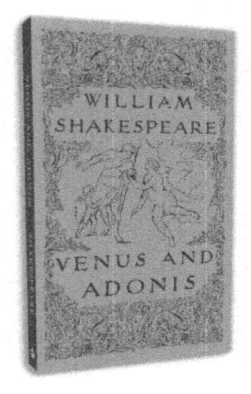

ISBN: 9781804470947
paperback
£5 • 80pp

ISBN: 9781804470916
paperback
£7.99 • 120pp

ISBN: 9781913724146
paperback
£8.99 • 128pp

ISBN: 9781804470305
paperback
£7.99 • 88pp

DISCOVER THE FULL COLLECTION AT
WWW.RENARDPRESS.COM